THE BEST JOB EVER

Fashion Designer

Ian F. Mahaney

PowerKiDS press.

New York

Published in 2015 by The Rosen Publishing Group, Inc.
29 East 21st Street, New York, NY 10010

First Edition

Editor: Caitie McAneney
Book Design: Katelyn Heinle

Photo Credits: Cover, pp. 3–24 (background design) Toria/Shutterstock.com; cover (girl) Robert Przybysz/Shutterstock.com; p. 5 catwalker/Shutterstock.com; p. 6 vipflash/Shutterstock.com; p. 7 (top) Diego Cervo/Shutterstock.com; p. 7 (bottom) Peter Bernik/Shutterstock.com; pp. 9 (top), 13 (both) Robert Kneschke/Shutterstock.com; p. 9 (bottom) Dragon Images/Shutterstock.com; p. 10 Africa Studio/Shutterstock.com; p. 11 BlueSkyImage/Shutterstock.com; p. 14 Lipnitzki/Roger Viollet/Getty Images; p. 15 (top) Martin Good/Shutterstock.com; p. 15 (bottom) Anton Oparin/ Shutterstock.com; p. 17 Cindy Ord/Getty Images Entertainment/Getty Images; p. 19 (main) Everett Collection/Shutterstock.com; p. 19 (inset) Hulton Archive/ Getty Images; p. 21 (top) Bloomberg/Getty Images; p. 21 (bottom) wavebreakmedia/ Shutterstock.com; p. 22 Syda Productions/Shutterstock.com.

Library of Congress Cataloging-in-Publication Data

Mahaney, Ian F.
 Fashion designer / Ian F. Mahaney.
   pages cm. — (The best job ever)
 Includes index.
 ISBN 978-1-4994-0130-1 (pbk.)
 ISBN 978-1-4994-0085-4 (6 pack)
 ISBN 978-1-4994-0104-2 (library binding)
 1. Fashion design—Vocational guidance—Juvenile literature. I. Title.
 TT507.M3484 2015
 746.9'2023—dc23
                              2014029746

Manufactured in the United States of America

Contents

FASHION DESIGNERS

Do you have an eye for fashion? Do you love mixing and matching new outfits and **accessories**? Do you like creating an original style for yourself? Then you might want to be a fashion **designer**!

Fashion designers plan the way clothing will look. Fashion design is a kind of art, but it's also closely tied to business. Fashion designers make sure their clothes and accessories are going to sell. They pay attention to the kinds of clothing that have sold in the past. Fashion designers follow fashion trends and create clothing that people will love to buy!

Fashion designers work with different colors, cuts, and **fabrics** to make one-of-a-kind pieces of clothing.

A CREATIVE CAREER

Fashion designers get to be creative at work, just like an artist. But instead of painting pictures, fashion designers **express** their creativity by making plans for clothes, shoes, or accessories. Some designers love art or drawing. They often **sketch** their designs on paper. Fashion designers also like sewing and knitting.

It makes some fashion designers feel accomplished when they share their designs with others. Some designers have their clothes shown in magazines or on a runway at a fashion show. They try to create the next big thing in the world of fashion. Some fashion designers even become famous!

DESIGNER BIO: MARC JACOBS

Marc Jacobs rose to designer fame in his early twenties. He worked as creative director for famous fashion company Louis Vuitton for 16 years. He also started his own companies—Marc Jacobs International and Marc by Marc Jacobs.

Many fashion designers do their work in a studio. It's a workspace that has all the tools they need to create their new designs.

DESIGN SCHOOL

Most fashion designers study design or similar subjects in college. Students learn about fabric, sewing, and color combinations. They learn how to illustrate, or draw, new designs and ideas. Students also learn about fashion history. Teachers in design schools often have **experience** working as fashion designers. They can help students apply classroom skills to fashion design jobs.

Fashion design students also learn how to design using a computer. This is called computer-aided design, or CAD. It allows designers to test colors and patterns on a computer without having to measure fabric and cut the pieces.

Design schools sometimes teach students how to recognize trends and how to forecast trends. Forecasting trends means guessing what will be popular soon.

MAKING A PORTFOLIO

Students studying fashion design usually put together a portfolio of their designs. A portfolio is a collection of samples to show employers. For example, a portfolio might show sketches, pictures, or CAD designs of clothing. Employers look at the portfolio to understand an **aspiring** fashion designer's skills. Portfolios also give employers an idea about the designer's personal style.

Portfolios show a designer's taste in clothing. While one designer might love many bright colors, another might like to use just one or two soft colors.

It's especially important for a new designer to have a portfolio because they have little experience. A fashion designer's portfolio is one of their greatest tools in landing their dream career.

WORKING YOUR WAY UP

If you're an aspiring fashion designer, you'll probably start with an entry-level, or beginner, job. You might get a job cutting fabrics and doing basic tasks at a design firm. You might get a job in marketing, or spreading the word about a fashion designer. You could also work as a **manager** in a clothing store to learn more about fashion.

After entry-level jobs, you might work your way up to something closer to a fashion designer. Design assistants work with fashion designers, and they help a designer's collection come together. They might help with fittings, making samples, and visiting factories or stores.

Students can begin their career working for designers through **internships**. Internships help them learn about making and designing clothes hands-on.

CLOTHING DESIGN

Designers make many different kinds of clothing, from ball gowns to bathing suits. Some designers focus on designing women's clothing, while others focus on men's or children's clothing.

Designers need to understand their shoppers. How much will their clothes cost? Who will buy them? Where will people buy them? A designer's clothing line might be bought by a department store or a boutique. A department store sells many different kinds of clothing, usually for men, women, and children. A boutique is a store that **specializes** in certain items. One shop may sell only bridal gowns or men's suits.

DESIGNER BIO: COCO CHANEL

Coco Chanel was a French fashion designer who opened her first shop in Paris in 1913. She designed a popular new style for women of the 20th century. Women still wear Chanel suits and dresses today.

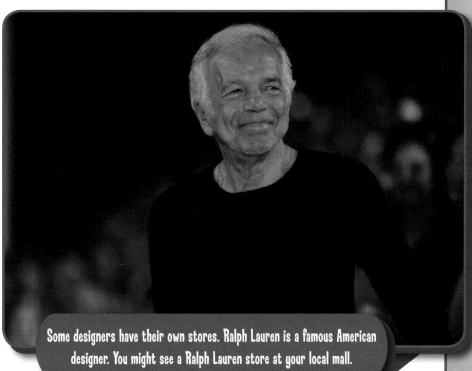

Some designers have their own stores. Ralph Lauren is a famous American designer. You might see a Ralph Lauren store at your local mall.

TIME TO ACCESSORIZE!

Some fashion designers focus their design efforts on accessories. Accessories include bags, shoes, scarves, and jewelry. Accessories add a special spark to a person's outfit. For example, someone might pair a black dress with red shoes and a white purse.

Like clothing designers, most accessory designers specialize in a certain area. Some fashion designers work only on purses or shoes. Jimmy Choo is a Malaysian designer whose shoes are well-loved. They're often featured in *Vogue*, a top fashion magazine.

Accessories are often designed to be ready-to-wear. "Ready-to-wear" means that the clothing or accessories can be bought right off the racks in a store.

Kate Spade is a fashion designer who designs many kinds of clothing and accessories, but she's most known for her purses.

THE PERFECT FIT

Some fashion designers focus on custom clothing. These designers make clothes that fit one customer perfectly. In women's clothing, this is called haute couture (OHT ku-TUHR). Fashion designers who make haute couture clothing are trying to set trends that ready-to-wear designers will follow. Fashion design company Versace might design a dress especially for a **celebrity**. When others see the dress, it might start a trend.

Similar designers called tailors make custom suits. For men, this is called bespoke tailoring. Bespoke tailored and haute couture clothing are expensive. That's because a tailor or designer spends a lot of time and money on each outfit.

"Haute couture" is French for "high fashion." In this picture, actress Jessica Biel wears a Versace gown to an awards show. That's an example of haute couture.

DESIGNER BIO: CHARLES FREDERICK WORTH

Charles Frederick Worth is considered the first world-famous fashion designer and the "father of haute couture." He was born in England in 1825, moved to France, and became one of the first designers to work on custom clothing.

JOBS IN FASHION

There are other jobs in fashion besides designers. Models pose wearing a fashion designer's clothing. They sometimes appear in magazines or walk the runway at a fashion show. Fashion photographers take pictures of the models. Many people work at fashion magazines, which play a big part in new trends. Some people create commercials and print ads for clothing. They place these ads on billboards, in magazines, on television, and on **social media**.

Other jobs in fashion include jobs in stores. Some people own boutiques or small clothing stores. Others manage large department stores. Buyers follow trends and stock store shelves with fashionable clothing their customers will buy.

If you like fashion, a good first job for you might be working in a store. Pay attention to all the different styles around you!

BREAKING IN TO THE BUSINESS

The fashion business is hard to break in to. It's hard to get a job as a fashion designer, especially as a beginner. It's often necessary to move to a fashion center like New York, Los Angeles, London, Paris, or Milan to get one of these jobs.

If you want to begin a career as a fashion designer, you can start working on it now. You can learn about fashion and fashion history in books. You can read about fashion trends in magazines. You can make crafts and draw custom designs. You can even learn to sew and make your own clothes. Show the world your style!

Glossary

accessory: Something extra that you add to an outfit.

aspiring: Strongly wanting to achieve a goal.

celebrity: A famous person.

designer: Someone who plans the way something will look.

experience: Knowledge or skill gained by doing or seeing something.

express: To let out feelings or ideas.

fabric: Cloth.

internship: An educational or training program that gives experience for a career.

manager: A person in charge of a business.

sketch: To draw.

social media: Online communities through which people share information, messages, photos, videos, and thoughts.

specialize: To focus on making or doing one kind of thing.

Index

Websites

Due to the changing nature of Internet links, PowerKids Press has developed an online list of websites related to the subject of this book. This site is updated regularly. Please use this link to access the list: www.powerkidslinks.com/bje/fash